Flesh, Tongue

poems

Yaya Yao

MAWENZI
HOUSE

We acknowledge the support of the Canada Council for the Arts for our publishing program. We also acknowledge support from the Government of Ontario through the Ontario Arts Council.

ONTARIO ARTS COUNCIL
CONSEIL DES ARTS DE L'ONTARIO
an Ontario government agency
un organisme du gouvernement de l'Ontario

Canada Council for the Arts Conseil des arts du Canada

Cover design by Peggy Stockdale

Library and Archives Canada Cataloguing in Publication

Yao, Yaya, author

Flesh, tongue / Yaya Yao.

Poems.

ISBN 978-1-927494-67-7 (paperback)

I. Title.

PS8647.A69F55 2015 C811'.6 C2015-905129-0

Printed and bound in Canada by Coach House Printing.

Mawenzi House Publishers Ltd.
39 Woburn Avenue (B)
Toronto, Ontario M5M 1K5
Canada
www.mawenzihouse.com

For my father,
Eugene Yong-Ging Yao,
who said he never got my poems

Contents

Cantonese Lesson 1: digits

back to where i never left, learning
the corners of feathered tongues. a friend is teaching me
to defend myself: my Cantonese is from 40
                                                  years ago when
                                                            my mother left

already the phone number i picked is all swearing:

gau chut chut gau
9779

yut ling say gau
1049

gau chut chut gau
cock   cock   cock   cock

yut ding say gau
definitely dead meat

Cantonese Lesson 2: past life

pok kai
drop dead

sei yan pok kai
dead one, drop dead

chut
cock

gau
cock

diu
fuck

chiu
screw, almost, like saying "chuck" instead of "fuck"

Q
like "kuck" instead of "fuck," but the roman letter when
written, and capital

hai
slutty, coquettish, flirtatious, forward

cheen sai
I must have done something in my past life to deserve this
feeling, yes
defended, ready to wipe
my tongue on a new city—
the minibus drivers on their mobiles

diu diu diu
echo my fresh technique
promise me belonging

where you're going

one ocean one
continent

from the place you were
born you are

dying, suspended
over university and elm

in february
with expert hands

chang ping aims into flesh long
needles

the tip
connects to
the point
opens into
the pathway and you
follow, she drapes a thin silk scarf over your trunk

leaves the room for a
tea from timmy's

she says to family

3 to 5 a.m. the body
is weakest

it will happen
then, he is
tired his body is not
holding water, call me
tomorrow

the path
you have taken:
shanghai to hong kong
hong kong to montreal
montreal to

toronto

parkdale to little portugal

little portugal to university and elm

university and elm to

                    3 a.m.
                    to 5 a.m. tides withdraw
from each meridian, that ocean

                    here to claim you, now you as always in
                    between

come 1: go home

(*lei*, lower departing tone)

From *How to speak Cantonese: fifty conversations in Cantonese colloquial; with Chinese character, free and literal English translations, and romanised spelling with tonic and diacritical marks, &c* by James Dyer Ball, 1902

come in
yup lei
come up, come not come?

I am coming,
you come
coming too slowly.

he is coming, coming
quickly. comes
flying comes

running comes

steaming comes
out,

come
back.

flesh, tongue

i don't know your   name
can't remember   the day you died
i can't honour you   with custom

long for you as   if i knew you
as if i never knew

you
i never knew   but there am i in
your
blood   before breath
running in   circles
of   let's call it
promise

and there are you   in mine
          i press against
my very flesh   you promised

a language
          with which to know you

Hokkien Lesson 1: the daughter's daughter's daughter's phrasebook

ang mo
red hair

jin sui
very beautiful

wah pah de leao see
I will beat you to death

wah zaii yah
I know

wah gaii gee
I can do it myself

strike 1: him, copper, bird

(*ta*, upper rising)

From *How to speak Cantonese: fifty conversations in Cantonese colloquial; with Chinese character, free and literal English translations, and romanised spelling with tonic and diacritical marks, &c* by James Dyer Ball, 1902

ta *strike*
ta k'ou *strike him*
ta kau *to fight*

ta *strike*
ta ngo *strike me*
ngo ta nei *i strike you*

ta t'it *strike iron*
(blacksmith)

ta t'ung *strike copper*

ta hoi

strike

open

ta sz

strike (to) death

ta

strike

tsok

bird

small heart dream, hong kong

down the valleys of penthoused mountains
chase your mother's girlhood shadows

you, another black-haired head
flooding the spaces between
concrete and everywhere
the flush of your first word

turning to the nearest
source, you open
up

you lean in

back across
the ocean, the sun is high

your mother wonders
what you think you'll find

go-down

(*lok*, lower even)

From *How to speak Cantonese: fifty conversations in Cantonese colloquial; with Chinese character, free and literal English translations, and romanised spelling with tonic and diacritical marks, &c* by James Dyer Ball, 1902

sai' sam lok
small
heart
go-down
'ho sheng lok
very carefully
go-down

Pomelo: For the son's son

Careful:
too much pomelo will give
you the runs

but the leaves of the tree
make the sweetest tea.

Cut the leaves and dry them on a roof
under the sun is best. The next day
steep the leaves, then leave
the tea to cool.

My grandma made it
for me as a child, she really loved me.

I was the only one. I was the son's son.

The only one surely blood.

strike 2: blood, sure

(*ta*, upper rising)

From *How to speak Cantonese: fifty conversations in Cantonese colloquial; with Chinese character, free and literal English translations, and romanised spelling with tonic and diacritical marks, &c* by James Dyer Ball, 1902

ta shou', lou ta fetch water struck by lightning
ta tin-sin send a telegram

ta t'am, ta chong to spy, to fight *or* to
battle
ta yeng to win
ta shong to wound, to be
wounded

english

see you fling it into the air
so far and never doubting it
will find its way back

stretch and flex and shimmy
shove
what do you think it's like
to trust every mouthful of it?

to not lead it down
paths with your palms
to the sky and your
back to the next
step squint
willing
the syllables
smooth as sibilance
of mother
tongues
suck slide
you closer to

the edge   of a drop
yawning

namelessness

does it feel like singing

1 music

entering silence
on silence's terms

2 music

crashing into quiet
like a foe

lake haiku

the spider waits
climbs, waits—an armoured tank slides across
a flawless highway

six weeks, no rain
the forest reaches down so deep
it keeps green

your head submerges
to face a sunken sun—skittered
silent syncopation

blue lake feeds our barest skin
with her own

July 2012

song: moving time

it's moving time
so move with me
to the boom of your heartbeat and mine

because here we are
shining, opening into
the truth of voice as it echoes
to claim the knotted
corners of the too-vigilant flesh

because here we are, loving
in the face of a dollar a day
on that railroad we collateral
damaged exploding on

slivered screens where they tell us
we're myth when we are
legend, dangerous
because we dare to love
ourselves whole
enough to know

it's moving time
so move with me
you move into you
i'll move into me
and together rejoice
to the boom of your
heartbeat and mine

sound

beneath throat, breath

beneath breath, earth

beneath earth, stone

beneath stone, liquid

beneath liquid, vein

beneath vein, fire

beneath fire, darkness

beneath darkness

the sound

of beneath

offering

ma and i are the
living here, negotiating
terrifying details under shallow
breath, the dead reluctant witness
to a stumbling thanks
giving:

a small pyramid of sunkist
oranges and a pear on
a red plastic lotus
stout-stemmed, edges
gold-painted

rectangles of gray marble stacked
eight high to fluorescent ceiling, on each tile
the face of an ancestor, behind each
we know
a sealed cubicle, a jar
of ashes

tofu and wheat gluten in
a styrofoam box, white / yellow / orange
mock chicken / pork / goose

with eyes our nerves race
to interpret, the ancestors
look at us from the damp depths
of the inadequacies we were so
relieved to find names for,
offering these again, should
the nerves disrupt, or
pressing tongues soft
against new

a borrowed vase half full of government
water and yellow chrysanthemums
in unison, three bows
three sticks of incense
a flame

ma cries, kneels to be eye-level to her father's
mother, father's
father. she wets a wad
of toilet paper with water from
a plastic coke bottle,
wipes the marble top to bottom:
the name of their hometown
their names
the names of their children

she tells them

we have flown back
to you from a gamble,
a destiny you willed us with your sweat.
after 40 years, and imagine you here,
now, the dust
of your bodies in cells
a low corner of a room crowding
with ghosts, i always meant to come
sooner, and here
here is my daughter

yes, this is our meeting place, and i am here
to give thanks:
laced fruit from california, flowers from guangdong

thanks for the tightness
in your muscles, built to give me better that i might

Teach Native English for 250 hong kong dollars an hour that i might
come here to touch your cool
stone

searching for

my

a

truth to speak to you
now

soon

we hear footsteps
the shuffle of fruit into plastic bag

sorry, the women say, we are closing

as we leave the grounds we see
them redistribute
the oranges to the elderly

the vegetarian food to the dogs

ma's eyes flame to mine and down

next time just fruit

Shanghainese Lesson 1: from the father's father

nong shao de
you know

nong ve shao de
you don't know

che veh
eat

go

1. grandfather's go

lucky
(to) a land packing dollar
i gave you

why are you here?

2. go (*Hou'*, upper departing tone)

From *How to speak Cantonese: fifty conversations in Cantonese colloquial; with Chinese character, free and literal English translations, and romanised spelling with tonic and diacritical marks, &c* by James Dyer Ball, 1902

no one has gone
have man gone (there are people going)
            to go good (it is well to go)?

I have not been
yet. go early or
late at night go
takeaway, go
take,
go get

tam hou'
carry it away (by one man, slung on two ends of a pole)

t'oi hou'
carry it away (between two men, on a pole)

t'ok hou'
carry it away (resting on one's shoulder, &c)

aspiration

wandering in
memory to look
for rotting things and hold
them against the light

at just the right angle, you could see
the quality of this rot, the qualities
of rot. the quality of this
thought, the qualities of
rot, do you
see?

that would make it all worth it.

I could call myself a poet, as I
pick through mountains
of mess, caressing potential
transcendence until
crushed or frozen,
dead.

down I: exert yourself

(*lok*, lower even)

From *How to speak Cantonese: fifty conversations in Cantonese colloquial; with Chinese character, free and literal English translations, and romanised spelling with tonic and diacritical marks, &c* by James Dyer Ball, 1902

lok hou'
go down

lok lik
down with your strength

lok teng
down bargain (pay money)

lok pun
down capital

lok pat
down pen
(write)

down 2 (*lok*, lower even tone)

From *How to speak Cantonese: fifty conversations in Cantonese colloquial; with Chinese character, free and literal English translations, and romanised spelling with tonic and diacritical marks, &c* by James Dyer Ball, 1902

lok ‘yu
down rain

lok suut
down snow

lok pok
down hail

lok
to fall

waterfall

for angel sinclair

the drop pulls
the current under
makes way for

you
thinning as you reach the edge

when all you can do

is give in to your weight
and know it

loosening
into some place lower down

when you meet
resistance you'll know
you're
there

at another kind of faith

surrender

cultural gaps

silence:

weakness	strength
beginning	friend
action	wall
contestant	end

aspiration 2

voice striking
air without
question or conceit

Cantonese Lesson 4: telling time in minutes, or, context

60 minutes is
yat goh chung tau
a clock head

30 is
buun goh chung tau
half a clock head

yat goh chee
a word is 5

yat goh gwat
a bone 15

three words can make a bone (I told you)
four bones a head (a revolution)
a body to bridge a certain
silence, new born to keep us
one, to invite

ancestors to sing
across a galaxy of three planets and a single orbit

second (a sliver of bone)
minute (a letter)
hour (a head that spins through stars)

to give away her wish
and the exact circumstances of your
birth

plans

1972
you left china believing
one day you'd come back

1981
show your children all
they had been
missing until

june 4, 1989
you knew you wouldn't

you taught thcm
all you could in the living
room over dundas

chinese flashcards, picture books

maps spanning 2400 years, an empire's bor-
ders shifting

you believed in your flesh despite the surplus
of cow's milk and wheat they ingested, despite
the distance from ancestral ashes
despite american tv

later you could tell them
you're not what
i expected

their bones,
your mutant hopes forever

calcifying, flesh
marbled with your
perplexed affection

Note: June 4, 1989 is the date of the Tiananmen Square massacre.

Mandarin lesson: departing

man zou
walk slow

wan an
night peace

zai jian
see you

Meditation for the sister's daughter's daughter

All my life, I've learned
happiness can't come from someone else.
I set out for it every day:
I hold my hand
listening to the air
in

out
to sense my destination

this beaten heart, unclenching
even
for a while.

Cantonese Lesson 3: not stomach

Have you eaten yet?
sik joh fan mei
eaten rice or not

Yes
sik joh
ate

Are you happy?
hoi mm hoi sum
open not open heart

Yes
hoi sum
open heart

Are you hungry?
toh mm toh ngo
stomach not stomach hungry

mm toh
not stomach

Are you thirsty?
hau mm hau hohk
mouth not mouth thirsty

hau hohk
thirsty, blistering in dry
heat, aching
to

sprout a tongue
or two, that will
quench you, new

sing you

in a melody blood remembers

true

come 2: dominion

(*lei*, lower departing)

From *How to speak Cantonese: fifty conversations in Cantonese colloquial; with Chinese character, free and literal English translations, and romanised spelling with tonic and diacritical marks, &c* by James Dyer Ball, 1902

not good come (do not come)
not come can (I cannot come)

horse coming, rain
coming, comes blowing, or blown here.

The boat comes—

came
came

Man comes, water comes, officer comes,
wind
comes. Dog comes.
Comes to-strike,
striking comes.
Struck.

Mouth: Her advice for the son's daughter

Pass, but don't
study too hard. Go
outside, breathe good
air, always breathe through

your nose. Tell your mother to check on
you at night, press

your lips

closed when you are sleeping,

never leave your mouth open.

It makes a girl look stupid.

city haiku

1. getting by

you breathe the breath
of faint firefly—making
out her moment

when to
be seen. when
not to

2. getting caught

pigeons push up against
the false scar—the city street

the bones it blankets
the bones it rises
to meet

enabling, enabled

a
            be, bled
a lean-able
                        deal,
                                    laden.
Land-able.

(Lend) bed.

                                        End
                                            end

end led.

                                            blend led, lead

land

                        be.

To do

Mrs Amador tends the turnip patch, a square
of green in upturned soil and winter sun:

My hands are useless, I
just make them.

My fingers are no good
any more, but I force
them to do.

Now everything takes so
long, but what the hell
can you do, you know.

Things just take time.

parkdale

does it have a
sound yet on your skin?
a city so far
from oceans

you cross
a highway to reach the
lake, watch the water
stretch so
far, waiting
for a feeling

to arrive
at your single room,
on the wall, a photo
of you with the people
you loved

meet your younger
eyes, ones that never
doubt that you, now
are doing what
you came

to do.

now
on your skin

for you to remember

tongue: multiple choice

member
tool
muscle
bone

landscape
soundscape
bitter
home

salty
sweet
sour
crone

tender
tending
edgy
loan

transplanted tongue, or, tongued

in this mouth
you fill and hollow

your dusty root twist
curled into the root
of my mother

tongue,
english,
sometimes
I can't hear myself
in you

dia/spore

how are   you

to

me

now, what are we

from

relations bloomed and
broken

by blood

by communion

by water

land

or air

mother tongue

without past or future
without fluency

without loyalty or vocabulary
without grace

without idiom or device
without imagination

i claim
you out of nothing
but hunger

in your nature
it is
to feed

Walk slow

When is your sound?
Where is your silence?
Why are your people?

What are your questions?

song: for my high school sweetheart

in that downtown
cold you appeared, scarves echoing wild rainbows
through concrete tunnels

telling me about your latest poem
your latest indecisive man
you'd shake your fist,
moan and laugh from deep as we
walked through teeming
streets, stretching
our mouths wide, waiting
to catch the red braid of
breath that would
take us
somewhere,

casting giant shadows on the doorsteps of bloor coffee shops
where hours later we were two teas
one coffee and 7 poems warmer

the days we sat in trees, like the one at christie pitts
that held us in her palm whenever
we asked

or alexandra park at midnight, where
you taught me how to inhale, and i lay
and lied: i think i'm feeling something

some nights as my smoke and silence
heaved itself into thick vomit,
fermented tears, your hand
resting behind my heart

we gave our songs to strangers on the rush-hour college
streetcar
2-part sweet honey in the rock
somebody come and carry me into a 7 day kiss
the time a man gave us $1.39, good job!
we bought coffee and laughed

my love

we laughed
my love

now listen now
that you fail to visit
even dreams

i've read your letters
i've listened to your mixtapes
i've written you poems and set them on fire
i still don't know who started it

find, if you do, a way to never let me
know

2002

Visit

canadian tire cameras catch you
buy a length of rope

a scrap of forest at the edge
of a suburban field named
for a bird i've never heard of
you choose a tree

a jogger in the morning
your hair
dew

much later, we visit
one evening, too late. we burn
the things we want to say to you, ourselves
something pushes us out

leaves cling to our jeans as we
slam car doors. we blast whatever's
on the radio. we look at windows, we
don't go back.

song: gift

we're in an unfamiliar
kind of love. you're my first.
there's nothing i can read to understand you
the air won't stop and i can't tell time.

you breathe in the belly of my
love, through your skin,
under water. you
are shedding a
fine hair while you
hear me now

because of what you'll need
from me and what you won't,
because of the risk you take in choosing us,
because all i can
do is all i can do,
i will be the mother who
shares with you not
blood, but destiny
not gene, but
legacy

to breathe the air
to look at the light
to cry

are you ready?

June 2013

YAYA YAO was born and raised in Toronto's Parkdale and Little Portugal neighbourhoods. Her poems have been published in several journals, including *TOK7* and *Contemporary Verse 2*. Her short play, *Tongued*, received staged readings through playwrights' units with Nightwood and fu-GEN Theatre companies, and she is co-author, with Helen Anderson, of the *Educator's Equity Companion Guide*.